Oliver Noble

Regular and skilful music in the worship of God

Oliver Noble

Regular and skilful music in the worship of God

ISBN/EAN: 9783337136130

Printed in Europe, USA, Canada, Australia, Japan

Cover: Foto ©Thomas Meinert / pixelio.de

More available books at **www.hansebooks.com**

Regular and skilful Music in the Worship of GOD,

Founded in the Law of Nature, and introduced into his Worship, by his own Institution, under both the Jewish and Christian
Dispensations;

SHEWN IN A

SERMON,

PREACHED AT THE

North Meeting-House, NEWBURY-PORT,

AT THE

Desire of the Church and Congregation,

FEBRUARY 8th, 1774

By OLIVER NOBLE, A. M.

Pastor of a Church in NEWBURY.

Printed at the Desire of the Musical Society,
In NEWBURY-PORT.

AND OF A NUMBER OF

Gentlemen and Ladies who heard it.

Then sang Moses and the Children of Israel this Song.   MOSES.
Come before his Presence with Singing.   King DAVID.
I will sing with the Spirit, and with the Understanding.   PAUL

BOSTON:

Printed by MILLS and HICKS, for DANIEL BAYLEY, in
NEWBURY-PORT, 1774.

DEDICATION.

TO the Church and Congregation that ufually worfhip in the North Meeting-Houfe, NEWBURY-PORT; and to the Mufical Society in faid Town; and to the Singing Men and Singing Women, wherever this fhall come;——This Sermon is humbly dedicated, by their moft

Obedient and

humble

Servant,

for Jefus's

Sake,

The AUTHOR.

A

DISCOURE on MUSIC, &c.

I. CHRON. xv. 22.

And Chenaniah, *Chief of the* Levites, *was for Songs ; he inſtructed about the Song, becauſe he was ſkilful.*

THAT the bleſſed God, the author of nature, the God of providence and grace, the Lord of angels and men, ſhould be worſhipped with praiſe and thankſgiving by all intelligencies, is founded in the moral and unchangeable fitneſs of things, and belongs to the religion or law of *nature* ; and will remain binding upon all moral beings, as long as the relation of Creator and creature ſubſiſts.

Our account of the duty of praiſing God with the voice of melody, or *ſinging* forth the praiſes of the ALMIGHTY, is *coeval* with *creation* itſelf. For when God had finiſhed the ſtupendious work of creation, and had taken, as it were, a *retroſpect* of the grand machine, and ſaw that *all* was very good, all ſuited to his divine and infinite *plan*, and had pronounced it ſo in the preſence of the

heavenly

heavenly *hoſt* ; the heavenly CHOIR celebrat-
ed the workmanſhip, and worſhipped and
glorified the inſinite Workman, in a *ſong* of
praiſe, as the moſt proper and ſublime way
of *praiſing*, and worſhipping God.

For, and on that great occaſion, the angels (who are called morning ſtars, and ſons
of God) *ſang together and ſhouted for joy*.
That is, they expreſſed their praiſe in a vocal
anthem.—And indeed, it ſeems to be a kind
of natural worſhip, that forces itſelf upon the
intelligent mind : The obligation to which,
ſeems to be written on the heart ; that has
always excited all moral beings, that have
had any true ſenſe of God upon their minds,
to expreſs their homage to him with their
voice in ſongs of praiſe. For we find the
people of God in the early ages of the world,
expreſſing their homage to God this way ; and
that before there were any poſitive inſtitu-
tions of God about this part of worſhip. This
is evident, not only from the account we have
of that memorable tranſaction at the Red Sea ;
but at other times, and on other occaſions.
Vocal Muſic is, in *itſelf*, a noble and ſublime
art, and anſwers ſublime purpoſes ; eſpecially
when it takes a ſerious and ſacred turn, and
is employed in the worſhip and praiſe of God.
It has not only been *revered, honored, learned,
and practiſed*, by the greateſt, wiſeſt, and *beſt*
of men in all ages, as that which ennobles the
foul

foul of man, raifes its ideas, and fweetly calms
the rougher paffions, and furprifingly prepares the mind for the fublimeft, and moft
vigorous exertions and meditations; but this
excellent art, has been introduced into the
worfhip of God by his *own* fpecial inftitution,
under both difpenfations : Which adds dignity to it, and gives weight to the *fubject* ;
and which fhould animate all that are capable
of it, to a facred ambition to learn, in fome
good meafure, this important art, and to get
fkill in mufic, efpecially in pfalmody ; and
to ufe it well, in the praife of their God, and
to the honor of their Redeemer, and to their
own, and others edification.

The bleffed God was long worfhipped by
facrifices, before he was pleafed to fettle their
number, kind, quality, and the manner of fa-
crificing as we find them in the Jewifh law,
inftituted of God, by Mofes, his fervant. So
it was with this part of worfhip of which we
are treating :—Though it is founded in the moral *reafon*, and unchangeable *fitnefs* of things,
and the obligations to vocal praife inforced
by the law of nature; yet God was pleafed to
give particular orders about it, and to regulate its form and *manner* by fpecial command
and inftitution. This he did in particular in
the time of David that great and excellent
King of *Ifrael* ; under that great *Mafter* of
divine *mufic*, the man after God's own heart.

The

The bleſſed God was pleaſed, as it were, to ſettle the muſical part of his worſhip, under the countenance and inſpection, of his favorite King ; *who* himſelf was the moſt *ſweet pſalmiſt* and ſinger of *Iſrael*. He therefore gave particular orders and directions about this ſublime part of the worſhip of the Lord in his *ſanctuary* ; that the ſacred ſong might be managed decently, and in order, to the honor of God, and to the edification of the pious and devout worſhipper. And to this end, a very conſiderable number, both of ſinging men, and ſinging women, were appointed, to lead in*, if not wholly to perform this part of divine worſhip. And they were to devote their time, and talents, to the employment, or to qualify themſelves for it. They were to make divine muſic, and the art and knowledge of it, their principal buſineſs. †
This was, that they might be *ſkilful in muſic*, and know how to manage the ſacred *ſong* in the beſt manner, that the praiſes of the Lord might be ſung in all its parts, in various chords and proportions of muſical ſound ; that it might be calculated, to ennoble the *ſoul*, to warm the *heart*, and to wrap every power in ſacred

---

* I am not certain but that the congregation of the Lord joined with the ſingers in the public worſhip of praiſe, under the Jewiſh diſpenſation, eſpecially thoſe whoſe voices were tolerably formed to muſic ; though a late ingenious writer is of a different opinion.

† This appears from their having a public maintenance allowed them, as the Prieſts had. *Neb.* xi. 23.

facred devotion. Though the inftructions about the divine mufic, that we find recorded in this chapter, relate more efpecially to a particular occafion, viz. that of bringing back the *Ark* of God, and fetting of it in the place that King *David* had prepared for it ; yet we find the fame care about the order and regularity of mufic, continued in the ftated worfhip of God, all along under the Jewifh œconomy. That it was not of human invention, or meerly by the command of *David*, the King ; but by the command of God, and having the ftamp of divine appointment, fhall be confidered in the fequel. What has been already faid opens the way for a more particular confideration of the text. " And Chenaniah, chief of the Levites, was for fongs." Can it be a queftion, what *fongs* thefe were, that he was to be mafter of, and to manage with *beauty* and *order ?* Surely no, the point is obvious ; they were the fongs and pfalms of the *Lord*, compofed by holy men of old, under the *guidance* of the Holy-Ghoft ; defigned and adapted to worfhip and glorify the God of Ifrael. And to this end, they had not only the fongs of Mofes, and others that were infpired by the facred fpirit, *fet to mufic* ; but David *himfelf*, the fweet finger of Ifrael, was moved by the Holy-Ghoft to compofe many divine pfalms and facred hymns, which he either *fet* to mufic himfelf

himfelf, or commited them to feveral fkilful mafters of mufic for this purpofe; that they might be fung with fkill, and made ufe of in the public worfhip of God.

Such a mafter of mufic was Chenaniah, mentioned in the text, and it is worth our notice in this place that he was *chief* of the Levites : That he fuftained one of the firft charaƈters for honor and dignity in the kingdom of Ifrael ; yet, notwithftanding, fo noble, fo excellent was the art of mufic, efteemed in that day, efpecially divine *mufic*, to be employed in the worfhip, and to the honor of the true and living God ; that the greateft perfonages of the age did not think it below their dignity to apply themfelves to, and fpend much of their time in the ftudy and practice of it.

King David *himfelf*, though one of the greateft monarchs of the age in which he lived, though he was poffeffed with a capacious mind, and was remarkable for his wifdom, for his prudence, as well as for his valor, power and authority ; was no lefs remarkable for his piety and clofe attachment to the worfhip of God and a moft fervent promoter of it in every part, and is *memorable* for his *fkill* and *zeal* in this excellent part ; that it might be performed by rule, with fkill, with decency and order, fo as to anfwer in the beft manner the good ends of its appointment.   And

And with this view was Chenaniah appointed maſter of the ſacred ſongs of the Lord ; in the original it is, he was a lifter up of the ſongs, it is, as if it was ſaid, that he was the moderator of the ſacred muſic, *i. e.* he not only directed about the tunes and parts thereof, compoſing ſome and chooſing others, adapted to the meaſure, nature and ſolemnity of the pſalm, and ſong to be made uſe of in the worſhip of God, on this, or that occaſion, ſo that the melody might be ſweet and engaging, ſuited to raiſe the ſoul to the higheſt pitch of devotion ; but he took pains with, and inſtructed the ſingers, how to lift up their voices *together* in harmony, on the various parts that he aſſigned them, ſo that the various notes ſhould *chord*, and afford the ſweeteſt muſic to the ear ; that by this means the divine inſtruction of the *ſong*, or the matter of the *pſalm*, might find the readieſt acceſs to the *heart*, and better the *ſoul* by raiſing it to God, and directing all the deſires and affections, to things divine and heavenly.

Thus much at leaſt, is ſuggeſted to us, by his being the lifter up of the ſacred ſongs of the Lord, and inſtructing about them, *becauſe he* was ſkilful. For this is the reaſon given, why he was aſſigned to this honorable employ ; why, he was appointed moderator of this part of God's worſhip, and to fit and qualify others for this excellent buſineſs, by

B   inſtructing

instructing them in this sublime art. It was *because* he was skilful ; *q. d.* he was well qualified to regulate the time and movement of the sacred song, because he entered into the spirit and design of this method of praising and worshipping the God of Israel ; not only so, but he well understood the scale of *music*, and was ready at the use of it, and *apt* to teach others the regular and harmonious performance of the duty, that it might be acceptable to God, and well answer the ends of its institution, with regard to men, their *comfort* and *edification*.

This short passage of inspiration affords us the following sentiments, which I think are either expressed, or fairly implied, viz.

That praising God with the *voice* as well as with the heart, or singing forth his praises with the voice of *melody*, and that with skill, gracefulness and harmony ; is a duty of great importance, and incumbent upon all that are capable of it : Founded in the moral fitness of things, enforced by the special institution of God, and binding upon the christian, as well as the Jewish church and people of God. That the duty is founded in the reason and unchangeable fitness of *things*, and taught us by the law of nature, may appear not only, from the relation there is between God and the creature, but from the *sentiments* and *practice* of men, on great and weighty

weighty occasions, while under the guidance
and direction of reafon, and natural confcience
only. Natural reafon without, and before
there was any pofitive inftitution of God,
about the matter, has proved *fufficient* to
teach men that they could no way fo properly exprefs the earneft defires and warm
emotions of their fouls, in pious gratitude and
joy, as in the fymphony of fong, and animating chords of mufic.

This is not only evident from many tefti-
monies that might be brought from profane
hiftory, but from the fketches we often find
in the facred records ; where we find that
pious men of old, without any fpecial direction of God about it, and *meerly* from the
dictates of their own minds ; on great and
animating occafions, break forth into finging,
and expreffed their religious thankfulnefs, in
fongs of praife to the Rock of their falvation.
This was undeniably the cafe with Mofes and
the children of Ifrael at the Red Sea ; *then
fang Mofes and the children of Ifrael this
fong.* And it does not appear, that as yet
there was any divine inftitution about this
part of the worfhip, but otherwife, that it
was the natural overflowings of their pious
joy and *thankfulnefs* on that great *occafion,*
and the dictates of reafon and natural confcience, that expreffed *itfelf* in mufic, and directed them thus to fing God's praife.

I

I might mention a like inftance at the *well of Beer*, where the people of God, being delivered from diftreffing thirft, brake forth into fongs of praife ; worfhipping the God of their falvation with vocal mufic ; and moft likely the fongs of Deborah, and Barak were of the fame kind. But I fhall not enlarge upon this thought.—I am next to obferve, that this excellent and fublime art of mufic, was introduced into the ancient church of God, by his own fpecial *appointment*, and made a neceffary and important part of his worfhip.

The great Creator of all things, having wonderfully conftituted man, with regard to the organs of fpeech and found, as well as on other accounts, forming his voice in fuch a manner that it is eafily *tuned* to various notes of concord and harmony ; and having impreffed his very nature with a confcioufnefs of ufing it in the praife of his Creator, was pleafed, in his own time and way, to give fpecial direction about it. And after he had erected a church in the world, and from time to time, had *revealed* his mind and will concerning his worfhip, and fhewn how he would be worfhipped, as well with regard to the *manner* as *matter* of WORSHIP, was alfo pleafed to give fpecial command and direction about this part of worfhip, directing that it fhould be performed in the beft manner, moft agreeable to the nature of the duty, and to the

nature

nature of man ; *i. e.* with fkill and harmony
of the voice : That it might tend to roufe
a fpirit of devotion in the mind of man, and
to elevate his foul in the praifes of his Creator
and Redeemer : And to this purpofe there
were a great number appointed to the facred
fervice, and were inftruded in the art and
fkill of mufic under the beft mafters of the
age ; that in the worfhip of God, it might be
performed without difcord or confufion, but
with decency and order ; for our God is a
God of order, not of confufion.

Now the obvious reafon, why fo much
fkill was to be exercifed in, and pains taken
about this part of worfhip was, to prevent
confufion and diforder, in a part of worfhip
where fo many were to lift up their voices together ; in a part, defigned and calculated to
reach inftruction to the foul, by the *harmony*
of Sound, and to warm the heart, in the exercife of true devotion ; which would be impoffible were it to be performed without rule,
fkill or order.—Now to evidence that all this
care and pains about the *mufical* part of God's
worfhip, which we find recorded in the text
and context, did not originate from the mere
humour of King David ;—but was by the appointment of the Lord, we need but turn you
to the books of Ezra and Nehemiah. For
upon the return of the captivity, in the days
of Ezra and Nehemiah, when the true worfhip

ſhip of God was again ſet up in Jeruſalem, and
the enquiry was *ſtrictly* made, what is that mo-
del the Lord commanded us, by Moſes and the
Prophets :—The Singers in the worſhip of
God were appointed in their order, according
as we find it recorded in the text and context ; and this is expreſsly ſaid to be as the
Lord had commanded, by the mouth of his
ſervants, the Prophets ; and again it is ſaid
that Jehoiada, the prieſt, appointed the
ſingers in the worſhip of God ; as *it was
written in the law of Moſes, and commanded
by David, the King* : All which refer to what
is written in our text, and context, and to
the regulation of the ſacred muſic, under the
man after God's own heart : Which is ſuffi-
cient to illuſtrate the point, that *vocal muſic*
was introduced into the worſhip of God, by
his own *inſtitution*; and that the Jewiſh
church were under not only moral, but *poſitive*
obligations, to perform it with all poſſible regularity and harmony, as well as with pious
frames of heart and religious exerciſe of ſoul.
. But if the queſtion ſhould ariſe, is this
binding upon *chriſtians?* Or ſhould any en-
quire, is it yet obligatory upon the church of
God under the chriſtian diſpenſation, to worſhip God with the voice of melody, in *ſinging*
forth his praiſe ? To which I anſwer, that
the affirmative is fully evident, and may be
clearly illuſtrated, both from the reaſons of
the

the inftitution, that ftill remain, and from the *pofitive* teftimony of God in this matter, found both in the old and new-teftaments.

Now, it is evident, that the reafons of the duty ftill remain, and always will, as to fub-ftance; though it may vary as to fome cir-cumftances.—The reafons of the duty, as to fubftance, are of a moral nature; originate . from the relation between the Creator and creature, and will always continue, fo long as that relation fubfifts. They depend upon the unalterable *fitnefs* of things, and therefore the reafons of the duty are unchangeable. Therefore it follows, that as the reafons and nature of the duty, were not peculiar, to the ftate and circumftances of the Jewifh church, but of equal obligation under every difpen-fation; fo muft of confequence, have equal weight with, and be equally binding upon chriftians. Now, one obvious reafon why *finging* with the voice of melody, was intro-duced into the Jewifh church, and by divine *appointment* made part of their religious wor-fhip was, becaufe that this facred *mufic* had a *ftriking* tendency, and peculiar force and *energy*, to elevate the foul of man, and to engage the mind in the moft fervent exercif-es of religion; and, as it were, to abforb it in the warmeft raptures of devotion.

For nothing perhaps (in a way of means) can have a greater tendency, to *affimulate* the
                                                    humble

humble foul to God, and more and more liken him to his bleffed image, and raife every power to the higheft pitch of gratitude, praife and thankfgiving : And facred *mufic* has evidently the fame bleffed tendency now, it had of old, and for the fame reafons ; for human nature is much the fame now, as it was then ; God is the fame yefterday, to-day, and for ever, and as worthy to be worfhipped and praifed as ever he was, and pious obligation to do it is the fame, and ftill remains ; fo that, that which was the obvious reafon for its being then inftituted, is as conclufive for its being now inftituted, and to continue bind-*ing* upon the chriftian church.

And if regular, fkilful, and harmonious managment of the facred fong, in all its parts and movements, had a tendency then to enkindle devotion, to warm the heart, and to animate the foul, as it were to the raptures of joy and gratitude ;—it has now, and for the fame reafons ; and it is as binding upon the *chriftian*, as it was upon the Jewifh church and people of God.

It is readily granted, that there were many things in the inftituted worfhip of God's ancient church and people, that were peculiar to them, and to that ftate and period of the church, and have no place under the chriftian difpenfation : And that becaufe the reafons of this appointment do not now obtain

tain, they being abolifhed by the coming and kingdom of Chrift.

Such were all things *purely ceremonial and typical,* which are now entirely done away by the coming of Chrift the antitype, and the introduction of the gofpel ftate. And indeed, it appears to me to be a very juft and fafe way of determining what things were ceremonial and what were not, what were peculiar to the then ftate of the church, and what were not ; by taking into our view the particular *reafons* of the inftitution.

For thefe practices and ordinances that had place then, *not* for REASONS that were peculiar to the Jews and that difpenfation, but for reafons that are of equal weight under every difpenfation, are no doubt *binding* under every difpenfation, and ought to be-conformed to, by every ferious worfhipper of God. This *reafoning* is applicable to the duty we are now confidering. Whatever circumftances may differ, yet the *fubftance* or *effence* of the duty, remains ftill the fame, and as binding upon us, as them ; and that with regard to the *general* manner, as well as matter of the duty, *i. e.* with *gracefulnefs and harmony,* as well as with grace in our hearts.—But further, the fame fentiment is *plainly* taught us in the word of God. There are feveral intimations to this amount in the old-teftament, that fuggefts to us that

C   this

this duty of worſhipping and praiſing God with the voice of melody, was to be continued under the goſpel diſpenſation; one or two of which I ſhall mention, that to me appear to imply a command, and to make the duty binding upon the church of God under the goſpel diſpenſation;—particularly in the 100th pſalm, *make a joyful noiſe unto the Lord, all ye* LANDS; *i. e.* ye people of all lands,—*ſerve the Lord with gladneſs;—come before his preſence with ſinging.* This we find is an addreſs to all PEOPLE, of *all* LANDS, and at *all* TIMES. It is *allowed* by all *commentators*, and by the Jewiſh *Doctors* and *Rabbies themſelves*, That this pſalm has a peculiar *reference* to the goſpel day, and ſtate of the church, and therefore, is a command to chriſtian worſhippers *to come before*, or into the *preſence of the* LORD, *with ſinging*, and to pour out the gratitude and joy of their hearts in *harmony of ſound, in the charming accents of ſkilful and well regulated muſic.* But it is time that I hint to you a few things, that will afford us further light in this matter, which we collect from the new-teſtament.

I ſhall but mention the ſongs of the bleſſed virgin, of Zachariah and Elizabeth, and of good old Simeon, and others, that vented the pious raptures of their ſouls, in *vocal* ſongs of praiſe; but ſhall more particularly conſider the *examples* and teſtimonies, that

Chriſt

Chrift and his apoftles have left us upon facred record. When the Lord Jefus, by his example and command, had inftituted the facrament of the holy fupper, at the fame time, did fignify, and fuggeft to us, that it was his will that we fhould fing his praifes, as a part of religious worfhip under the gofpel difpenfation : For he concluded the important, the inftructive celebration with a facred hymn.—Should it be objected, that this is the only time we have any account of our Saviour's finging as a part of divine worfhip, and fo it cannot be argued from thence, that he would have his church *fing* as a part of religious worfhip : In reply we may obferve, that we have no account of his celebration of the holy fupper at any other time; what then ? He no doubt left the whole for our imitation, and hereby fully fuggefts to us, that it is his will that we fhould worfhip him by finging forth his praife.

Neither have we any account of his praying before, or after his fermons, What then ? Why no doubt he was a conftant attender on the Jewifh temple worfhip ; of which finging was a conftant and important part, *equally* known, and equally binding as the duty of prayer, or any other part of divine worfhip.

But it will be to our purpofe to *comment* a little, upon what we find in the writings of St. Paul, relating to this duty of *finging* the
praifes

praises of God in our worship ; especially see to this purpose the 14th chapter of his first epistle to the Corinthians.—And it is observeable here, that the professed design of this chapter is to regulate the worship of God, so that it might be performed decently, and with order, he aims to reform several irregularities in the worship of God, that had so soon crept into the church, that the *christian* worship might be guarded against confusion and disorder ; and managed with that decency and order that would have a tendency to promote the declarative glory of God, the honor of the Redeemer, and the *mutual* edification of *christian* worshippers. And it is in this connection that he says, *I will pray with the spirit, and I will pray with the understanding ; I will sing with the spirit, and I will sing with the understanding* : And he does not say this only with reference to himself, as what he resolved upon with regard to his own conduct, but this is what he enjoined upon the whole church of God in his name, speaking with the authority of an inspired apostle.

And it is much to our purpose, and worth *particular* notice, that we find this great apostle speaking of *singing* as a well known part of religious worship, in common and stated use and practice, equally known and acknowledged with either praying or preach-
ing,

ing, and a duty equally binding upon the chriftian church.

And here he lets us know that it fhould be performed not only in the fpirit, but with the voice, not only with a right temper of mind, and with true devotion of heart, but with *underftanding* : Not only with underftanding as to the matter and meaning of the facred *fong*, but as to the *rule* and manner of its performance, *i. e.* with fkill and harmony. This glofs upon the words is eafily juftified, from the fimilitude the apoftle brings to illuftrate his argument, which is taken from the defign and ufe of a trumpet in war ; for if the trumpet gives an uncertain found, who fhall prepare himfelf for the . battle; *i. e.* if the trumpet give an irregular, confufed, or uncertain found, it throws the foldiers into confufion, and diflerves the caufe which it was defigned to promote.

So it is with the vifible worfhip of God in all the parts of it, if the whole affembly be fpeaking or praying at one time, or all together, or in an unknown tongue, it introduces confufion ; though we hear the found the underftanding is not inftructed, and the heart cannot be bettered ; the affections are not excited, devotion and piety are not promoted. The fame is obferveable with regard to finging the praifes of God ; (the defign of which part of worfhip is, that our voices

may

may be lifted up together) there muft be fome known and determinate method, or mode of found, well underftood, in which we can unite, or it cannot anfwer the purpofe of edification : Therefore the praifes of the Lord are to be fang forth, not in *uncertain* founds, not in confufion and diforder, with the harfh and jarring notes of difcord ; but with harmony and concord, underftanding the manner, as well as the matter of the facred fong.

For if, in finging the fongs of the Lord, we do it in irregular and uncertain founds, where is the harmony ? How fhall we fing together ? How fhall we keep time and movement together in this part of worfhip ? How fhall we underftand one another ? And how is it poffible that we fhould be excited hereby to devotion, and be mutually edified.

So it appears that by *underftanding*, the apoftle means *fkill* in the *manner*, as well as underftanding in the *matter*, to be fung in the worfhip of God ; and anfwers to inftruction and fkill, mentioned in the text.

To the fame purpofe is that of the fame apoftle to the Coloffians, iii. 16. where the duty now under confideration is exprefsly enjoined upon all chriftians in common, under the gofpel difpenfation, viz. that they teach and admonifh one another, in pfalms, hymns and fpiritual fongs, *finging with grace*

in

in their hearts unto the Lord. Though in this paffage of fcripture, a gracious temper of mind is enjoined, the neceffity and importance of grace in the heart inforced, in order to the right performance of this duty; which indeed is the leading fentiment in the right performance of every duty. Yet he cannot mean to exclude the harmony of the voice, for the end aimed at depends upon its being vocal; which is teaching and admonifhing *one another:* The external part of the duty is taken for granted as a well known part of worfhip; but here the apoftle reminds us of the better and internal part of it, viz. Grace in the heart that fhould always accompany the external performance of the duty, as the beft method, in order to anfwer the great and important end of the duty; teaching and admonifhing one another, that is, by ftirring up gracious affections in ourfelves and others, by the elevating accents of *mu-fic* in fongs of *praife*, and by the united harmony of voice. Now it is evident this end cannot be anfwered without finging together in a focial manner, and fkilfully uniting our voices in the folemn, in the inftructive fong:

Thus have I fhewn that the duty of praifing God with the voice of melody, or finging forth his praife in fkilful and well regulated *mufic*, is binding upon the chriftian church

and

and people of God, as much as it was upon
the Jewifh, and is taught us in the fcriptures
both of the old and new teftaments. But
perhaps it will be expected that on this occafion fomething fhould be faid, more particularly. concerning the manner, decency and
order of this part of divine worfhip.

We have fhewn already in this difcourfe
that *finging* the praifes of God as an act of
worfhip, is a duty taught us, both by reafon
and fcripture ; but how frequent it is to be
practifed or how often we fhould *fing* praife
when we come together for worfhip, is no
where pointed out in the word of God. But
it is to be a part of our public worfhip, and if
fo, why not a part of our family worfhip
for the fame reafons, it has the fame bleffed
tendency to warm the heart, and to excite
fpiritual devotion in the family as well as in
the houfe of God. Since therefore the duty
itfelf is clearly taught us in the word of God,
and the frequency and fome other circumftances are not, chriftian prudence muft direct ; but reafon and conftant experience of
the benefits of it, urge us to frequency in
this foul-cheering and heart-animating duty.

But further, I fhall obferve, that in the
compofition of this difcourfe, I have attend-
ed to fome fcripture intimations that have
convinced my mind more than ever of the
propriety of beginning our public worfhip
with

with a fong of praife. That before mentioned paffage in the 100th pfalm fuggefts
as much, *come before* his prefence with *finging* ; which words in their plain and obvious
meaning, naturally lead us to conclude that
finging fhould be our firft employ when we
come into the prefence of the Lord ; that
we fhould begin his worfhip with this fublime
and holy exercife ; but let us take the fourth
verfe in connection with the firft, and the
latter will ferve as a comment upon the former, *enter into his gates with thankfgiving,
and into his courts with praife* ; which I
think fully intimates to us, that when we
come into the courts of the Lord, we fhould
begin his worfhip with a fong of praife :
The reafon and nature of the thing fpeaks
the fame language, and points out the propriety of beginning the worfhip of God with
finging, when we can with any conveniency
and decency of voices ; for this duty devoutly
performed, has a powerful tendency to compofe and folemnize the mind, and to raife the
affections, and thereby to fit and qualify the
foul, for all fubfequent parts of worfhip.

The thought I leave for the ferious confideration of all God's people.

But further, as *finging* is a part of God's
appointed worfhip, no doubt it aught to be
performed, with the moft *decent* and *reverend*
pofture of the body : For we are to offer unto

God,

God, in his worſhip, the *body, as well as ſoul and ſpirit, which are his.* This duty is an immediate addreſs to God, and that equally with prayer ; and why ſhould we not ſtand up to worſhip God, in this duty, as well as in that ;—unleſs want of health, or bodily ſtrength prevent, which will equally warrant us to ſit in the duty of prayer, and no more in one duty than in the other : Will any object the fatigue and wearineſs to the body ; ſuch may do well to conſider, that this was the cry of old.: What a wearineſs ! What a wearineſs !—And it is obſerveable that their character was none of the beſt ; beſides the natural advantage of a ſtanding poſture in this part of worſhip, as it gives play to the lungs and advantage to the voice, there is a moral reaſon for it ariſing from our obligation to offer unto God our very ſelves (as the apoſtle expreſſes it) both in ſoul, body and ſpirit, which is but our reaſonable ſervice.

And now I will appeal to the common *ſenſe* of mankind, whether ſtanding in an immediate addreſs to God is not moſt becoming the duty.

We often read of their ſtanding up to ſing, and they ſtood up to praiſe the Lord in the beauty of holineſs, &c. But no where as I remember of their ſitting down to ſing forth the praiſe of the Lord.

But further, it is a fair deduction from what has been ſaid of the uſe and end of ſacred

muſic

mufic ; that it fhould be performed with fkill, and harmonious modulation of the voice. The fentiment is fully taught us in the text and context, and in other parts of the holy fcriptures. This part of divine worfhip of old was performed with fkill and harmony of the voice, and there was great care and pains taken that it might be fo ; and to this end was Chenaniah appointed moderator of the facred fongs of the Lord : He was *fkilful* himfelf, and inftructed others to be fo, that this part of worfhip might be performed with gracefulnefs and harmony. Now fkill in any thing implies a rule, according to which that fkill is to be exercifed ; and inftruction fuppofeth, the being taught this rule ; and the ufing and applying of it fkilfully to the purpofe defigned.—So finging in concord and harmony, or fkill in *mufic*, neceffarily implies a *rule*, and that they perform it fkilfully, are acquainted, in fome good meafure, with this rule ; and apply it to the purpofe defigned, with gracefulnefs of voice, and harmony of found.

Mufic has its foundation in the nature of things ; it takes its rife from the unalterable proportion of ʃoᴜɴᴅs one to the other ; all the variations of notes and changes of the voice or inftrument in *mufic*, are ftill dependant upon the foundation, *i. e.* the *invariable proportion of* ʃoᴜɴᴅs. It depends upon

as

as exact proportions, as any part of mathematical *science* whatever, of which it is an important part. And therefore is pleafing and edifying fo far, and no farther, than it is compofed by, and performed according to that rule, and exact proportion; the farther from it, the more diftant is the found from *mufic*; but the nearer to this, proportion, and the more *exactnefs* in performing, the more excellent and *charming* the mufic; and of confequence the greater power and influence upon the human mind; and the greater tendency to excite pious affection, and true devotion in the worfhip of God.

It hath pleafed the great Author of nature, not only fo to form and conftruct the human voice, as that it may be, in general, eafily formed to the *rule* and *fcale* of mufic, whereby we are rendered capable of making melody to God, with our voices; but hath formed in us, the curious organ of the ear, a faculty whereby we are capable of diftinguifhing the fweet chords and accents of well proportioned *mufic*, from the jarring notes of diffonance; and to be highly delighted with the one, and not lefs difpleafed and difgufted with the other : For the ear tryeth founds, as well as words; therefore, that the facred mufic ufed in God's holy worfhip, may be both pleafing and edifying (for one it cannot be without the other) it muft be performed with regular

exactnefs

exactnefs of found, time and movement*.
As far diftant, as it is from this, fo much it
loofeth of its power and influence to pleafe
and

* In order further to illuftrate this thought, and to throw
light upon the fubject, I fhall favour the public with fome
critical remarks of my worthy friend and brother, Mr. Strong,
of Simfbury, the only author I had read upon the fubject, and
to whom I am indebted for feveral fentiments in this difcourfe,
though I truft I have fo far digefted them, and wrought them
into my own method of thinking and fpeaking, that they have
fo far become my own as that neither he nor others, can ac-
eufe me as a plagiary. I fhall therefore extract fomething from
his piece by way of marginal note, as it is wrote with great
juftnefs and ingenuity, and better expreffes the thought that I
am now confidering, than any language of my own ; but let us
hear what Mr. Strong fays upon the point ; he, fpeaking of
the ground and foundation of mufic, as founded in the *nature*
of things, takes this inference, " Is it true that mufic has its
foundation in the nature of things, and depends upon exact
proportion ; and as to its effentials always remains invariably
the fame ; then certainly the principal and fundamental rules
by which it is taught are alfo the fame in all ages. Whenever
therefore a regular attempt is made to reform pfalmody, it is
not to introduce properly a new way of finging, but to reco-
ver men from their errors, and to bring them back to practice
upon the only good old way : And whoever difapproves of,
or oppofes fuch an attempt through diflike, does fo through
ignorance or fomething worfe. Yet this, notwithftanding, when
people have been long without a regular method of finging in
the worfhip of God, and have departed from it, it is not at
all to be wondered at, if many warmly oppofe an attempt for
a reformation, through an averfion to innovations in matters of
divine worfhip, and the more precife and confcientious perfons are, the warmer their oppofition ; and yet all through ignorance or miftake : Such has always been the cafe with refpect to reformations of all kinds, in things pertaining to religion or the worfhip of God.---Again,---Though the rule be
one and the fame, yet it may be differently applied, and as to
non-effentials, very perceptable alterations and variations may
take place, perhaps in all cafes ; for inftance in finging, the
notes ufed in mufic may be founded flower or quicker, longer
or fhorter, being juftly proportioned, and the rule effentially

and delight the foul, and to excite it to, and animate it in the exercife of true devotion. Therefore from hence follows the importance of acquiring fkill in facred mufic, that our voices may be lifted up together in all the parts of the facred fong; and that with as great exactnefs, and with as much harmony as poffible. There are many paffages in facred fcripture, that reprefent God's approbation of the fkilful and melodious performance of this

the fame. In former times, the longeft note was to be founded four times fo long as the longeft now in ufe: So that although it be effential to good *mufic* that the feveral notes have their proper founds, yet as to the length or continuance of their founds, it is not of the effence of mufic, but of its circum-ftantials, and may therefore be varied. Alfo with refpect to keeping time with utmoft exactnefs, in all the feveral *parts* of the *tune*; this is fo effential to good finging, that it cannot poffibly be good without it; of the truth of this every one is witnefs, who has any tafte for mufic: He quick perceives the difagreement, and finds his ear wounded whenever it is want-ing; though others who have not that tafte, difcern nothing of it, and therefore are by no means competent judges in the cafe. But the methods ufed to meafure and keep the time ex-actly have been different, in different times and places; and it is but a circumftantial thing, what method or motion be ufed, provided it be decent and well anfwer the end. The prefent method of beating the time, as it is called, has been found the moft eafy and exact of any hitherto tried among us. The ex-cellency and beauty of mufic, and I add its tendency to anfwer the purpofes of religion, much depend upon giving the founds properly, and keeping the time with critical exactnefs. All the cavals and objections that can be thrown in the way, againft regular finging, will go but very little way towards convincing any one who has a tafte for mufic, and finds himfelf tranfport-ed almoft to rapture, by its fweet harmonious ftrains, that re-gular, well proportioned mufic has nothing in it preferable, to the finging we have been wont to have, while we went without rule."

this duty of singing forth his praise; I shall mention but one or two. When King Solomon conveyed the ark of the covenant of the Lord to the temple he had built for it, and sat it in the designed place for its rest, he did it with a band of music, the most grand and sublime that we have any account of; and it is worth our notice, that when the singers, sang all as one, and when all the instrumental music coincided with the vocal, so as to become all as *one*, *i. e.* in perfect concord and harmony; that then, and not till then, the glory of the Lord filled the house; and the cloud of glory which was the cymbal and token of the divine presence and favour, so covered the ark, and the mercy-seat, that the priests could not stand to minister, because of the glory and perhaps because of the exstatick rapture of their souls in holy devotion, 2d Chron. v. 13. which see, &c. and God has often appeared for his people and given them signal deliverances, in consequence of the devout singing of his praise. "When the singers that were appointed to go before the army of Israel, in the time of Jehosaphat, when the Moabites invaded them; sang and praised the Lord, saying, praise the Lord for his mercy endureth for ever, then the Lord appeared for them, and wrought a great salvation." I might mention the instance of Paul and Silas, and other instances

of

of God's gracious interpofition upon his peoples, worfhipping of him with fongs of praife; but time would fail : All which intimates to us thus much at leaft, that the bleffed God, has always been, and is now, ready to give gracious tokens of his approbation and favour, to the exactnefs and harmony of this part of his worfhip, when accompanied with gracious exercifes of fpiritual devotion. And that in this way he is ready to grant us the mercies we need, common or fpecial ; not that this fkilful and harmonious finging the praifes of the Lord, procures his favour, or moves the heart of God towards us ; no verily, he is infinitely and unchangeably difpofed to mercy and kindnefs. But this exercife greatly prepares and qualifies the foul for the receipt of mercy ; all which confiderations fhould be improved as a powerful motive to excite us to qualify ourfelves for, and to take great care and pains in the performance of this part of God's worfhip, as well as in all others ; for God is a God of order, and will be worfhipped decently and with order; as well as in fpirit and in truth.

But to conclude the thought, which indeed has been carried through, and interwoven with the whole difcourfe, we may obferve, that this fublime part of worfhip, of which we are fpeaking, ought not only to be performed with fkill, and with engaging melody

of

of the voice, but with grace in the heart, it
ought in all reafon, to be a gracious melody;
it muft be accompanied with fpiritual, warm
and elevated devotion of the foul. This indeed is the primary end of the inftitution :
Though the outward regularity and beauty
of pfalmody is that by which God may be
vifibly glorified in the church; yet the outward eloquence of mufic in religious worfhip is chiefly defireable, as it has a powerful
tendency to ftir up gracious affections, and
to promote the religion of the heart. Therefore we fhould always have the moft folici-
tous concern, that we not only fing graceful-
ly and mufically with the voice, but with
grace in our hearts, making melody in our
hearts to the Lord; that we may glorify
God in our fouls, bodies, and fpirits, which
are his :—However ufeful and neceffary the
former is, yet it is fo chiefly as a mean and
tendency to the latter; for without this we
fhall fail of acceptance with God, and lofe
the fpecial benefit to our own fouls; and in
the iffue be found, but as founding brafs, and
a tinkling cymbal; and all our mufic be
turned into mourning, fad lamentation, mi-
fery and woe : But what remains is by way of
A P P L I C A T I O N.

I. From what we have heard upon the
fubject, we infer the manifeft reafon we have
thankfully to acknowledge; and pioufly to ad-
mire, both the wifdom and kindnefs of our

E   great

great Creator, in forming us capable of fo excellent an art, fo divine an employ as that of
mufic, efpecially facred mufic, to be ufed in his
own worfhip. Our God it is that hath adjufted
the invariable proportion of founds, and giv-
en thefe chords of mufic power to ftrike our
minds with the fweeteft furprife, and moft
agreeable rapture ; he hath formed the ear,
and given us the fenfe of hearing, whereby
we quick perceive its force and energy—are
greatly delighted with it, and find it reach
inftruction to the *heart* ; and that it carrieth
our fouls to God, on the wings of faith,
love, and holy defire.—Surely then thefe noble faculties, fhould not ruft with the talent
hid in the earth, by the flothful fervant, nor
be improved to the difhonour of him who
gave them ; but in return for the favour,
they fhould be improved to his honour and
glory, in *finging* forth his praife in holy *melody*, and fpiritual Song.

II. We infer from the fubject, that vocal
praife fhould alfo make part of our family
worfhip ; and every family ought to be capable of performing it with gracefulnefs and
harmony of voice, that is capable of performing any focial worfhip at all ; it is true
indeed, that the deaf, the dumb, and the
idiot are excufed for want of capacity ; and
perhaps a few whofe voices are fo weakened
with infirmity or age, that they cannot join
in the focial praifes of their God, which I am
fure

fure will be a great grief and burden to the
ferious and pious mind. And it is to be con-
feffed, that there is now and then one to be
found, who are in full ftrength, and of good
capacity for other employments, whofe
voices are fo ftubborn and *unwieldy*, as that
it is next to impoffible to form them to the
fcale of mufic, or learn them to fing any
part of the tune, let them take ever fo much
pains ; but this is not commonly the cafe.—
When this is the cafe with any one, it is his
unhappinefs, and he ought to be pitied ;
fuch perfons muft join their ears and hearts,
in this part of worfhip, but not their voices.
But the beft mafters of mufic tell us, that
there are but very few voices but what may
be tolerably well formed to the fcale of mufic, on one part or the other ; and a fkilful
mafter will quick perceive which part the
voice is formed for, and will direct them ac-
cordingly. So it appears that but very few
indeed, can excufe themfelves, in the neglect
of the duty we are confidering, either in
public or family worfhip. The fame reafons
that inforce the importance of finging with
the voice of melody, in the public worfhip
of God, hold good with regard to the worfhip of the family :—Has it a tendency to
excite devotion and to promote the religion
of the heart, in the public worfhip of God,
it has the fame tendency in the worfhip of
the family : and God is glorified in the lat-

Now what excufe can we make in the neglect of this part of worſhip in the family?
The common excufe made, we have heard
is, in its own nature, criminal:—We cannot,
we do not know how, we never learned to
fing, &c. This (unlefs the incapacity be natural, as we have before obferved) is your
blame, your inability, your incapacity is of
a moral kind, in which lieth your blame.—
Why have you not learned to fing? And
why have you not taught your families to
fing forth the praifes of their God and Redeemer? Have you not voices for other occafions? And have not your children voices
to ufe in finging wanton fongs? And have
not both parents and children, as well as
others of the houfhold, capacities to learn
other things much more difficult to learn
than pfalmody? Is not the true reafon why
you cannot manage a pfalm or hymn in the
family with decency and regular harmony,
to the glory of God, and your own comfort,
becaufe you will not afford yourfelves or children time, and a little expence, that ye may
be able to fing together, and offer to God
this part of his worſhip. If this is the cafe
guilt lieth at the door, you will have to
anfwer for talents mifimproved, or hid in a
napkin, if you continue in the neglect.
When we confider with what eafe a tolera-
ble acquaintance with the fcale of mufic
may

may be obtained in this day, fufficient to join in this part of God's worfhip, both in public and in the family, with decency and harmony : One would think that fhame muft cover the face, and blufhing the cheek of many, that neglect and difregard this duty, upon the plea of incapacity. I have dwelt the longer upon this inference, becaufe it is of great importance ; if the people of God would accuftom themfelves to finging in their family worfhip, they would foon find the ufe of their voices, they would foon be animated to learn the rule of finging, they would foon find the comfort and enjoyment of it, and we fhould foon fee an amazing alteration for the better, in our mufic in the houfe of the Lord.

III. But further we infer, that it is both the duty and intereft of every one, and that the obligation is binding upon all that are capable of it, now forthwith to apply themfelves to this noble art, and that with a view to the glory of God, in' the graceful and decent performance of this important part of his facred worfhip, that pfalmody may be revived among us ; indeed this will have a powerful tendency to revive dying and decaying religion among us, for we have heard that facred mufic has a peculiar influence on the mind of man, to foften the rougher paffions, to calm the whole foul, and to prepare

pare it for the moſt ſerious meditations ; and
in this way to prepare it for the grace of
God in the operation of his holy ſpirit, in its
converting as well as quickning influence.
It has been an old obſervation of the people
of God, that vital religion, the power of
godlineſs and pſalmody, have decayed and
revived together ; and cannot ſome of us
witneſs to ſomething of this ſort within our
own obſervation : And is not this an argument of weight, to excite us all to the moſt
vigorous attempts to revive declining pſalmody among us. And to this end it is greatly incumbent upon parents and heads of families, to take all proper care and pains to
be qualified for the performance of the duty
themſelves, and to ſee to it, that their children and houſholds are put under good ad-
vantages to this purpoſe : Have you not ſo-
lemnly covenanted with God, have you not
ſworn before many witneſſes, is not the oath
of God upon you, that you will train up
your houſholds in the *admonition* as well as
nurture of the Lord ? And God has appointed ſinging his praiſes in a ſocial way, as *one*
method of admoniſhing, Coloſ. iii. 16th.
St. Paul ſays, *admoniſhing one another in
pſalms, hymns and ſpiritual ſongs* :---You
therefore have not diſcharged this duty as
you ought, until you have made effectual
tryal of your capacity for ſacred *muſic* your-
ſelves,

felves, and given your children and others under your care, opportunity and advantage for it, where, and when, it may be had within your power, But

IV. Let high and low, rich and poor, chriftians of every denomination, ftation and relation of life, be perfuaded to put to their fhoulders in fo good a work, as the revival of facred *mufic* : As it cannot be done without labour and pains, and not commonly without fome little coft, let thofe that have voices, and can learn, efpecially the younger part, take pains in this excellent art, and let others, *efpecially* thofe that are opulent, contribute to this good defign as God has given them increafe, and as the caufe may require ; whether they mean to learn or not, that others may have all poffible advantage, who may he difpofed to apply themfelves to the bufinefs of learning the art of mufic, to be employed in the worfhip of God ; it is of public *utility*, and a public fpirit will excite to this. This is a flourifhing, opulent town, and it would be no great burden to fupport a free and open fchool, for the learning of facred mufic, a great part of the year ; and were this come into, the whole town would foon feel, and would quickly be convinced of the general benefit ; it is much to your advantage at home, and to your honor abroad, that you have not only made ample provi-
fion

fion for the fupport of the public worfhip of God in other parts of it, but have taken LI-BERAL care for the fchooling, and training up children and youth at the public expence *.

And will you be wanting in this part of inftruction that demands fo little expence, and is of fuch public and divine advantage ? I charitably hope you will not : If you would have the fpirit of pfalmody make rapid pro-grefs among you, let the rich and honorable, perfons of diftinction, of both fexes, engage in it, as well as others, and let none be too big to learn fo excellent an art, and fo fhall your example redound to the glory of God, and general benefit in this regard. It is no difhonor to the moft dignified perfon among us, to be engaged in facred *mufic* ; it is a genteel accomplifhment for the honorable of both fexes, and has always been efteemed fo by the wifeft and beft of men in all civilized nations : It will recommend you as men ; but how much more fo as chriftians ; it en-larges the mind, it ennobles the foul, it fil-leth it with refined fentiments, and turns but from the mind low grovling ideas. But above all, it is to the glory of God, and ferves your beft, your religious intereft, and will you not be perfuaded by this ? Are you more honorable than King David, are you

more

* There are three public fchools in Newbury-Port, fupported with handfome falaries, befides a very confiderable number of private fchools.

more refpectable than Chenaniah the chief of
the Levites : And they thought it no difhonor to make this facred mufic much of
their employ ; and in this heavenly art they
could inftruct others, and think it no ftoop,
no tarnifh to their honor.----Befides, ye rich,
ye honorable in this world, will ye not be
willing, by and by, to join iffue, and fing
in confort with thofe that are now beneath
you, when they, leaving the church mili-
tant, fhall join the church triumphant, and
eternally fing forth the praifes of God in
heaven. When perfons of diftinction, wealth
and honor, come to be engaged in fo good a
work, then there will be an open fchool or
fchools for pfalmody, upon a generous plan,
free for all denominations without diftinction ; and I cannot but flatter myfelf, that
this will foon be the cafe : And are there any
Chenaniahs among you, that are able to inftruct about the fong, becaufe they are fkilful, and are they willing to fpend their
ftrength, time and talents in the work, let
a fufficient number be employed in this bufinefs, and let them have a reafonable, and
but a reafonable reward. Then, and perhaps not till then, fhall we fee facred mufic
generally revived, and God be worfhipped
in our religious affemblies with the fweeteft
harmony in fongs of praife ; and our hearts
thereby be warmed with the moft fervent
devotion.   F   A

A thought or two more and I have done:
How melancholy is it, that we fcarce hear a
female voice in our public worfhip of praife,
though they make up fo great a part of our
worfhipping affemblies.—Suffer me, therefore, an addrefs, ye females of this large
and refpectable affembly, efpecially to the
younger part of you :—For *what* did the
great Author of *Nature* throw peculiar *fweetnefs* into your Voices, as well as delicacy
in your general conftitution ?—Why did he
form it upon a different and fublimer key ?
Why has he given it the force of *charm ?*
Was it to trill a loofe air, or chant a wanton fong ; to excite defire, and to give fuel
to the loofer paffions ?—Surely no.—Was it
not rather that you might ufe the fweetnefs
of your voice in finging the praifes of your
God, and to the honour of your Redeemer ;
and that by a diftinct part of the mufic, in
the public worfhip ; you might add *dignity*,
foftnefs and the *fweeteft harmony* to the folemn fong. It is worth your confideration,
that though the infpired apoftle feems to
have fhut your mouths in every other part
of public worfhip, yet he hath left them open
in this ; and will you fhut them in the only
part of public worfhip, in which you can
open them with decency, and to your own,
and others comfort and edification ? Will you
not improve the *liberty* God hath given you,
and

and in a peculiar manner fitted you for, *harmony* of found, and to grace the worſhip of his praiſe ; your imaginations are quick and lively, and by induſtry and application, you may ſoon learn, in a good meaſure, this excellent art ; and ſo your *charming* voices ſhall add beauty to, and give inſtruction in the worſhip of God. Had I time I might perſuade you to the duty, by many affecting arguments, by the conſideration of the redeeming mercy and dying love, by the bowels of a Saviour, who wept, agonized and died, that you might rejoice and ſing ; I might perſuade you by the frequent appearances of a gracious God, in diſpenſing ſpecial ſaving mercy in anſwer to praiſe, as well as prayer.—But I forbear.—Let me cloſe with a general addreſs, and perſuade all that can, to engage in, or promote ſacred muſic, by the *excellency and tendency of it*, as it raiſes the ſoul to God, and excites holy deſires after him, and the tokens of his favour, and calms the ſoul, quiets the rougher paſſions, and prepares the mind for ſerious meditations, and for the *reſidence* of God by his holy ſpirit ; it muſt be excellent ; and thus it is an excellent antidote againſt Satan's injections and temptations, whether ſubtle wiles, or fiery darts. Sacred muſic is a barrier to keep Satan out of the ſoul, it ſhuts, as it were, againſt him each avenue to the

heart ; mufic is in direct oppofition to this fubtle adverfary, he cannot live where it is, in any perfection, he muft flee before the pious and harmonious mufic of the people of God ; David's mufic could diflodge him from Saul himfelf, where he had long pof-feffion : So my friends, if you will unite in a gracious harmony of heart and voice, you fhall keep the devil out, or drive him from your hearts, you fhall drive him out of town, what I mean is, that ye fhall triumph over his temptations, through the promifed aid of him that hath loved you, and died for you ; by this, every litigating party may be foothed into love, peace, and harmony.--- Wrath, malice, evil fpeaking and backbiting, thofe tools and engines of the devil, and promoters of his kingdom, fhall flee before your united facred mufic ; while you meet together for this heart-chearing, and love and peace begetting and promoting employ : Thefe angry, turbulent paffions fhall find no place, for they fhall be foothed and hufhed to filence, by the practice of this facred art. The malicious heart, the angry paffions up-on a flandering backbiting tongue, *fet on fire the courfe of nature ; and are fet on fire of hell.* But the fofter and manly paffions, love, peace, joy, gratitude and friendfhip, are fet on fire *mufic*, and thereby neigh-bourhoods and communities are cemented
in

in the bonds of love and affection. Then
furely this heavenly art is worth taking fome
pains about ; it is a laudable ambition, to
fhine in the knowledge and practice of it,
and by thefe arguments would I perfuade
you to the fublime employ. But I fhall fhut
up the whole by turning your attention to
fomewhere between fifty and an hundred
motives, to learn and practice this excellent
art * ; there they are before you ; and it
affords me no little pleafure, to obferve that
thefe motives are, a number of them, of the
feminine, as well as of the mafculine gender :
---How are we charmed when they fing in
confort, how does the fkilful, and divine mufic *thrill* through every pore and vein ; and
how are our fouls wrapt in facred devotion.
O what would the mufic be, how ftriking
and inftructive the harmony ; could a whole
affembly fing with like exactnefs. Go on
my mufical friends and profper, and may the
Lord be with you, and blefs you ; fee to it
that you get the melody of the heart, the
grace of God, and true fpiritual devotion
there ; that from fweetly finging together
here, ye may join the church triumphant,
and the eternal anthem to God and the lamb
in the heavenly ftate.---And oh ! That the
facred fire may catch from man to man, and
from

---

* About the number of the fociety of fingers, that were prefent on the occafion.

from houfe to houfe, until it burn to a glo-
rious flame. May the laudable ambition, to
learn this fublime art, fpread through the
whole town, and into the neighbouring
towns and parifhes ; and may there be many *Chenaniahs* raifed up, who fhall inftruct
about the fong, becaufe they are fkilful.
Which may God of his infinite mercy grant,
through Jefus Chrift, Amen.

F I N I S.

www.ingramcontent.com/pod-product-compliance
Lightning Source LLC
Chambersburg PA
CBHW021435090426
42739CB00009B/1481